SOCCER'S
Greatest Clubs

Chelsea
FC

Fiona Young-Brown

Cavendish
Square

New York

Published in 2020 by Cavendish Square Publishing, LLC
243 5th Avenue, Suite 136, New York, NY 10016

Copyright © 2020 by Cavendish Square Publishing, LLC

First Edition

Website: cavendishsq.com

This publication represents the opinions and views of the author based on
his or her personal experience, knowledge, and research. The information
in this book serves as a general guide only. The author and publisher have
used their best efforts in preparing this book and disclaim liability rising
directly or indirectly from the use and application of this book.

All websites were available and accurate when this book was sent to press.

Library of Congress Cataloging-in-Publication Data

Names: Young-Brown, Fiona, author.
Title: Chelsea FC / Fiona Young-Brown.
Other titles: Chelsea Football Club
Description: First edition. | New York : Cavendish Square, 2020. | Series: Soccer's greatest
clubs | Audience: Grades: 5 to 8. | Includes bibliographical references and index. |
Identifiers: LCCN 2019013233 (print) | LCCN 2019016437 (ebook) | ISBN 9781502652690
(ebook) | ISBN 9781502652683 (library bound) | ISBN 9781502652676 (pbk.)
Subjects: LCSH: Chelsea Football Club--History--Juvenile literature.
Classification: LCC GV943.6.C44 (ebook) | LCC GV943.6.C44 Y68 2020 (print) |
DDC 796.334/640942--dc23
LC record available at https://lccn.loc.gov/2019013233

Editor: Kristen Susienka
Copy Editor: Rebecca Rohan
Associate Art Director: Alan Sliwinski
Designer: Joe Parenteau
Production Coordinator: Karol Szymczuk
Photo Research: J8 Media

Printed in the United States of America

TABLE OF CONTENTS

Chelsea players celebrate winning the 2017 Premier League Championship.

INTRODUCING CHELSEA FOOTBALL CLUB

London's Chelsea Football Club (or Chelsea FC for short) is one of the world's best-known and richest soccer teams. It is known for spending lots of money to bring talented players to the club. It is also famous for its turbulent, or rough, history that has led to its impressive successes in the twenty-first century.

CHELSEA: CHAMPIONS

In May 2012, Chelsea FC met FC Bayern Munich at Munich's Allianz Arena for the UEFA Champions League final. Sixty-two thousand fans packed the stadium. Hundreds of thousands more watched on television sets around the world. They all wondered, who would come out on top of Europe's premier tournament? Bayern had the home advantage. Furthermore, they already had four such wins under their belt. Chelsea had only reached the final once before, in 2008, when Manchester United had defeated them.

The teams seemed evenly matched. Neither scored until late in the second half. Bayern took the lead, only

Chelsea fans gather in the stands at Stamford Bridge during a match between Chelsea and the Wolverhampton Wanderers in 2019.

for Chelsea to make the score equal a few minutes later. The match ended in a 1–1 tie and entered a penalty shootout. Didier Drogba took Chelsea's fifth and final penalty kick. It landed in the goal. Thanks to Drogba, Chelsea defeated Bayern Munich and won the UEFA Champions League final.

The win placed Chelsea in an exclusive group. The team was one of only four teams to have won three major UEFA Cup competitions. It was the only English team to have done so at the time.

A LONG ROAD TO SUCCESS

For Chelsea fans, the road to success had been a long one. Many in the soccer world have often viewed Chelsea as the young upstarts in the game. The club has been described as a "nouveau riche" team rather than part of the "old Establishment." However, the truth is much more complicated than that. Chelsea has long enjoyed a certain celebrity status among the London soccer clubs. Its rise to success has been helped enormously by an influx of investment and heavy spending on talent, both domestic and international, over the last few decades. To think that Chelsea is relatively new to the game, though, overlooks a lengthy history.

Chelsea Football Club was founded in 1905. At the time, soccer, although hugely popular in the north of England, was still finding its feet in the south. Despite the name, the club is located in Fulham, which is a London neighborhood next to Chelsea. Another nearby team had already taken the name Fulham, so team organizers decided to name their club Chelsea.

John O'Hare (*left*) and Jackie Horton (*right*) were both players for Chelsea in the first half of the twentieth century.

ALWAYS POPULAR WITH FANS

From its earliest days, Chelsea was a popular team. The team attracted huge crowds to its home matches at Stamford Bridge Stadium. In the early days of the team's history, safety regulations did not limit the number of fans in the stadium. Crowds of fifty thousand were not uncommon. In fact, before World War I, crowds often reached this size. One match in the 1930s is believed to have attracted almost eighty-three thousand. Some say that as many as one hundred thousand actually crammed into every available space. Popularity was not a problem for Chelsea—nor was talent necessarily an issue. Almost immediately, Chelsea gained a reputation for bringing in well-known players from other teams.

There was still a problem, though. Despite immense popularity and some strong talent, Chelsea couldn't find a way to achieve much success. Somehow, during the early decades of its history, the team never seemed to blend. Chelsea couldn't quite win consistently. To be fair, the team reached its first FA Cup final in 1915, a mere ten years after being founded. The FA Cup is the oldest soccer competition. It started in 1872 and takes place between English soccer teams. Chelsea was the first London team to reach the final, where the team lost 3–0 to Sheffield United. However, Chelsea would not win its first major trophy until forty years later. In 1955, Chelsea finally topped the league for the first time.

Even then, success never stuck. Some seasons were filled with victory and happy fans cheering in the stands. Others were marked by big failure and relegation (being dropped out of the league). However, Chelsea's popularity continued. The club provided Saturday afternoon entertainment for generations.

Eventually, the loyalty of fans would be rewarded. Over the years, many famous players have worn the Chelsea blue. Jimmy Greaves, Frank Lampard, and penalty-scoring Didier Drogba are among the most famous. Chelsea has risen to become not only one of the top European teams, but also a global powerhouse.

Chelsea manager Ted Drake (*center right*) congratulates captain Roy Bentley (*center left*) on Chelsea's 1955 League Championship win.

A LONG HISTORY

Over one hundred years old, Chelsea FC is far from a new arrival to the English soccer scene. It's been popular with fans since it began in 1905, but the club spent many early decades struggling to get the success it wanted. Today, it is among the best teams in the world.

This recognition, like the 2012 UEFA title, has been anything but an overnight success.

Of course, a soccer team is more than just its players. Chelsea has seen many different managers, all hoping to lead the team to success. David Calderhead served the longest, managing the team for more than twenty-five years. Many others have stayed in the job barely one year, with Danny Blanchflower in the job for less than ten months and only thirty-two matches. Each of the many managers at Chelsea has become a part of the team's history. People like José Mourinho, Glenn Hoddle, and Ruud Gullit have been as vital as the players to building Chelsea into the world-famous team that it is today.

The team has also faced difficulties off the pitch. In the early days, the stadium was filled with cheering

Frank Lampard (*left*) chases the ball in a match against Spanish team Real Betis in 2005.

fans. By the 1970s, some of these fans got a reputation for violence and fighting. While Chelsea was struggling to win matches, it was also trying to end fan-related conflicts that seemed to follow them. At the same time, the team often faced money problems. Sometimes, players were not paid for weeks. However, Chelsea has overcome all of these challenges to become a top soccer club.

SPORT SHORT

In 1905, the year Chelsea FC was founded, important world events included a revolution in Russia.

The Chelsea FC team from 1905 poses for a team photo.

CHELSEA'S HISTORY

Most soccer clubs find enough players to form a team first, and then they find a place to call home. Not Chelsea! It was one of very few teams to have been built for a stadium.

CREATING CHELSEA FC

It all started when a businessman named Henry Augustus Mears came across a stadium at Stamford Bridge. The ground was built in 1877, to be home to the London Athletic Club. By 1904, Mears saw that it would be the perfect place to play soccer. At the time, soccer was very popular in northern England. It was not so popular in the south. However, a number of clubs existed in London. Mears felt that it was just a matter of time before soccer became popular in the city. It made sense to him that Stamford Bridge should be the home for a team. But which team? Stamford Bridge was located in the London neighborhood of Fulham. There was a Fulham team, but they played somewhere else. They weren't interested in moving, so on March 10, 1905, Mears and a group of men met at a local pub and

decided to create their own team. Chelsea Football Club was born. The name was chosen for the nearby neighborhood of Chelsea.

The next step was to recruit players. The club owners decided that they should buy some popular players rather than just rely on locals. Scottish defender John Tait Robertson was brought in to manage the team for its first season. Meanwhile, the goalkeeper and captain roles were assigned to William Foulke, a professional soccer player and cricketer. Foulke was known for his great height and his great weight. He is believed to have weighed more than 300 pounds (136 kilograms). He had also built a reputation around his temper. He argued with opponents, teammates, and referees, even walking off the field sometimes. The owners of Chelsea knew that this behavior actually made people want to come and watch games. Crowds wanted to see what he would do. To build a fan base, Chelsea had to get people to watch, and Foulke certainly grabbed people's attention.

In May, the team was elected to the Second Division of the English Football League. This is particularly noteworthy since the team had not yet played a game. In fact, Chelsea was the first team to be admitted to the league without having played.

Chelsea's first competitive game took place on September 2, 1905. It was an away game, and Chelsea lost 1–0 against Stockport. However, the team was gaining more fans. This was because of the number of famous players on their team and not the players' success on the field. During the club's very first season, a Good Friday match against Manchester United drew an estimated crowd of sixty-seven thousand.

At the end of its second season, Chelsea was promoted to Division One, the top level of English soccer. By this time, more well-known players had been introduced, including George Hilsdon. Hilsdon was nicknamed the Gatling Gun because of his "rapid fire" (or gunlike) ability to score goals. During his six seasons with the club, he scored 108 goals.

Manager Robertson had left after one season, as did his replacement, William Lewis. In 1907, David Calderhead took over as manager, remaining with the club until 1933.

LACKLUSTER PLAY AND WARTIME

In 1913, Chelsea gained its first foreign player, Danish Olympian Nils Middleboe. "The Great Dane," as he was affectionately called, worked in a bank and even said that he preferred his banking job to playing soccer. Because of this, he only played home games. He never traveled to away matches. Even so, he earned a great deal of respect from fans during his eight seasons with the club.

Although Chelsea reached the FA Cup final, a top competition, in 1915, the team lost. The remainder

Danish soccer player Nils Middleboe, also called the Great Dane, is shown here.

of the decade was unremarkable, although this was partly due to World War I. No matches took place while the war was happening. The 1920s were no better, and in 1924, the team was sent back to Division Two.

Chelsea would not return to Division One until 1930. Its return coincided with the Great Depression, when soccer provided a welcome distraction for the public. Some of the highest crowd sizes at Stamford Bridge were recorded during the 1930s. In October 1935, over eighty-two thousand people crammed into the stadium to watch Chelsea play Arsenal, another London team with whom they had a growing rivalry.

The outbreak of World War II interrupted regular league play again. However, it was important to maintain good spirits at home. The teams all played local matches and formed small regional leagues. Some players were fighting overseas, so famous players and celebrities often took their places at games.

Surprisingly, Stamford Bridge was not damaged by wartime bombing. After the war, it was the first stop for a visiting Moscow team on a goodwill tour in 1945.

The match ended in a 3–3 tie, with the third goal being scored by Chelsea's newest star, Tommy Lawton. The center forward set a new club record during his first season, scoring an impressive twenty-six goals. Despite his goal-scoring abilities, the team finished the season in fifteenth place. Lawton soon became frustrated. After just two seasons, he moved to another team.

In 1947, Chelsea FC was now more than forty years old and faced an ongoing problem. The team had lots of players who were talented, famous, and able to draw a loyal crowd of fans. Season after season, though, the

Chelsea fans watch as players emerge for a home match at Stamford Bridge in 1955.

team never seemed to reach its potential. For all its talent, Chelsea lacked the ability to play together as a successful team.

SETBACKS AND BUILDING A NEW TEAM

In the early 1950s, soccer was a dominant sport in Europe. It had established leagues, divisions, and national teams. Chelsea was among the top clubs, but that decade brought some challenges.

In 1950 and 1952, Chelsea suffered two FA Cup semifinal losses against Arsenal and only just avoided relegation, or being moved to a lower division. It was time for a change.

In April 1952, new manager Ted Drake arrived. He had formerly played for both Arsenal and England's national team, and it was hoped that he could turn around Chelsea's fortunes. Drake decided that the team's image was more focused on entertainment than loyalty. He wanted an end to the celebrity and a focus on results. Since the club's start, the image of a Chelsea Pensioner war veteran had been used both as a team nickname and on their jersey badges. This was now dropped. They were renamed "the Blues" because of the color of their jerseys.

There was no magical overnight success, but the team made steady progress under Drake's leadership. Within a few years, Chelsea won the League Championship. This made them qualified to participate in the first-ever European Cup in 1955. However, the English Football League (EFL) said that doing so might

RUUD GULLIT

When player-manager Ruud Gullit led Chelsea to win the FA Cup in 1997, it was important for many reasons. It was Chelsea's first major title for twenty-six years. Meanwhile, Gullit was the first foreign manager, as well as the first nonwhite manager, to earn a major trophy in English soccer.

Ruud Gullit holds up the FA Cup after his team's win in 1997.

Born in the Netherlands and of Surinamese ancestry, Gullit became as famous for his dreadlocks as he did for his remarkable soccer skills. He started his career in 1978, playing for HFC Haarlem. By 1987, he was World Soccer Player of the Year and joined AC Milan for a record fee of £7 million ($9.2 million).

Gullit joined Chelsea as a midfielder in 1995 and became the team's manager in 1996. He was the first Dutch manager of a Premier League team. Within one year, his team had FA Cup success. Although he left in 1998, he has said of his time at Chelsea: "Nice game, beautiful stadium, great crowd. It was the only time I really had fun."

In 2004, Ruud Gullit was listed among the Top 125 Greatest Living Footballers.

cause "fixture congestion and foreign contamination." As a result of EFL influence, Chelsea turned down the invitation. Its League Championship success proved to be short-lived. By the next season, many of the older players suffered injuries. Just one year after winning the championship, Chelsea dropped to sixteenth place.

Drake took an active role in player training and created youth teams. His hope was to find and develop young talent for the future. Instead of spending money on bringing in established stars, he concentrated on finding up-and-coming players from the lower leagues and amateurs who would work hard to win. Youth teams are a big part of Chelsea today.

One young star from the youth squads was Jimmy Greaves. By the time of his twenty-first birthday, he had already scored 100 goals for Chelsea. Many still

Young star Jimmy Greaves moves through the action against Tottenham Hotspur in 1957.

consider him one of the best players in the nation's history. With a tally of 132 goals in 169 appearances, Greaves moved to Milan, Italy, in 1961. Drake was then replaced by Tommy Docherty. Docherty brought in five new players.

Docherty's team was now much younger; the average age of the players was just twenty-one. Games were more fast-paced, and the team showed greater consistency, reaching three consecutive FA Cup semifinals. In 1967, they played against local rivals Tottenham Hotspur, informally called "Spurs," in the FA Cup final. This team defeated Chelsea 2–1. The loss stung all the more since the star players for Spurs had both played for Chelsea—Jimmy Greaves and Terry Venables.

FA CUP SUCCESS DOESN'T LAST LONG

The 1969–1970 season ended on a high note when Chelsea won its first FA Cup after beating Leeds United in a rematch. This win meant the team qualified to play for the 1971 European Cup Winners' Cup. This was a special game played between winners of different cup competitions. After beating Manchester City in the semifinal, Chelsea went on to beat Madrid in the final, but the success didn't last long. There were frequent arguments between management and players. As a result, there were always people coming and going from the team. By the middle of the decade, Chelsea had once again been relegated to Division Two. The club also had growing debts. Things were falling apart

quickly, and the years that followed were a yo-yo of promotion and relegation.

By 1980, the team was stuck in Division Two and had gone through three managers in four years. To make things worse, there was a fan problem. Chelsea's crowds had dropped drastically. Barely six thousand fans came to one match in 1982, a far cry from the days of sixty thousand cramming into the stadium. There was a rising problem of violence among some fans, worsening the club's reputation. The players were not being paid. Morale was at an all-time low. It was doubtful that the team would be able to make a comeback.

Hope rose again when Ken Bates bought the company in 1982. He paid just £1 ($1.33) and in return took over a club that was risking relegation to Division Three and its debts. His new manager, John Neal, took charge of on-pitch matters. Bates fired several players who were not performing to expectations, but with a minimum budget, finding replacement players was not easy. Despite the challenges, he added six players to the team in 1983.

The new team seemed to instantly connect. It won its first match 5–0 and easily made its way to the Division Two Championship and back into Division One. Sadly, John Neal had to step down due to poor health.

In 1985, John Hollins took over, followed by Bobby Campbell in 1988. Players started to leave, and within four seasons, the team found itself back in Division Two.

As on so many previous occasions, there were plenty of good players with Chelsea. The difficulty lay in getting them to play well together as a team and getting the team to consistently repeat its successes.

STRUGGLING ON AND OFF THE PITCH

As the 1980s drew to a close, Chelsea was still struggling on and off the pitch. Stamford Bridge was old and in need of modernization. It also needed to be bigger if the club was to give off a professional, successful image. Several years earlier, plans for refurbishment, or remodeling, hadn't developed into any change. Now the stadium was owned by property developers, and legal battles for control of the stadium added to the club's massive debts.

However, the final decade of the twentieth century was filled with hope for Chelsea. Two new players had been recruited, each of them costing £1 million ($1.3 million). Dennis Wise and Andy Townsend were the most expensive players in the club's history at that point.

Things began to look more positive again in 1993. Glenn Hoddle was a former England soccer star-turned-manager. As manager of Swindon Town, he had won that team's promotion to the Premier League. This new league had been formed in 1992 when the English Football League remodeled its system. Instead of

Divisions One and Two, there were now the Premier League (the top twenty teams), the Championship (the next twenty-four clubs), and then Leagues One and Two. Hoddle's arrival at Chelsea helped to raise the profile of the club and slowly win back the fans. His first season ended with Chelsea meeting Manchester United in the FA Cup Final in 1994. Although the team lost 4–0, it was making steady progress. The following year, Chelsea reached the semifinals of the European Cup Winners' Cup. Then came a trio of big buys. Dutch player Ruud Gullit arrived from Italy; Mark Hughes transferred from Manchester United; and Romanian Dan Petrescu donned a blue shirt. It didn't take long for fans and critics to claim that Gullit might be the greatest player in Chelsea's history. He was so popular that when Hoddle left in 1996, Gullit took over leadership of Chelsea. Although manager for only a few seasons, Gullit had an excellent ability to spot soccer talent. He brought in some strong players from Italy and France. This rising team of international players defeated Middlesbrough 2–0 in 1997 to win the FA Cup. After more than ninety years, Chelsea had claimed its place as one of England's top clubs.

Gullit left in 1998, but this time, the team was able to maintain its winning momentum. Just three months after he left, the team beat Middlesbrough again to win the Football League Cup, known then as the Coca-Cola Cup. Chelsea then defeated Stuttgart 1–0 and won the European Cup Winners' Cup. A win against Madrid for the UEFA Super Cup rounded out a very successful year. Chelsea's reputation was now impressing soccer audiences throughout Europe.

RIVALS: TOTTENHAM HOTSPUR

Chelsea first played fellow London club Tottenham Hotspur in December 1909, beating the club 2–1. However, their rivalry took off in 1967. It was the first FA Cup final to feature two London clubs and was nicknamed the "Cockney Cup Final." That's because many of the players on both teams had a Cockney accent. Tottenham won, but the result was especially painful since the Spurs team included Jimmy Greaves and Terry Venables, two former Chelsea stars. Later, Tottenham would narrowly avoid relegation to Division Two in the 1974–1975 season, but only at the expense of Chelsea.

The rivalry often became violent. After a tie in the 2007 FA Cup quarterfinals, fans clashed in a bitter fight that left ten people injured. Chelsea beat Tottenham in the 2015 Football League Cup final, and once again, violence broke out between fans. The following year, when the two teams played at Stamford Bridge, both clubs received fines after players fought on the pitch. There has been less fighting between the fans in recent years, but the on-pitch rivalry is likely to continue for years to come.

Chelsea's N'Golo Kante makes a move for the ball against Manchester City at a game in 2018.

KEY WINS IN CHELSEA HISTORY

3

As of 2019, Chelsea has an impressive trophy cabinet that includes eight FA Cups, six League Titles, five League Cups, two Cup Winners' Cups, one Champions League, one Europa League, and one Super Cup. Only four of these wins happened before 1990, and the majority of them have taken place since Roman Abramovich bought the club in 2003. In fact, Chelsea won the most major trophies of any club in England during Abramovich's first fifteen years. In this way, Chelsea is very much a modern success story.

SUCCESS IN 1998

After Ruud Gullit left in February 1998, striker Gianluca Vialli took over as player-manager. Such a midseason upheaval might disrupt many teams. However, Chelsea had been improving under Gullit; his leaving the team was reportedly due to an argument with club chairman Ken Bates rather than the team's performance. Chelsea continued to play well when Vialli took over. The team finished fourth in the Premier League but had been knocked out of the FA Cup in the third round. It was elsewhere that Chelsea would shine that season. In March, the club faced Middlesbrough at Wembley for the League Cup final. Chelsea won with two goals scored in extra time. Chelsea then went on to play Stuttgart in May 1998 for the UEFA Cup Winners' Cup. A second-half goal saw the team win and earn a place in the UEFA Super Cup match, held in Monaco in August. Chelsea defeated opponent Real Madrid 1–0, thus starting the 1998–1999 season on a high note.

THE DOUBLE

In the twenty-first century, the team has continued to prosper. One of their more notable successes involves the double.

Only a few teams in English soccer have won the FA Cup final and the Premier League title in the same season. This accomplishment is called the double. To win the double is considered a sign that the team is one of the best in the sport. Chelsea is the most recent team to have won the double, winning both titles in the 2009–2010 season—the team's eighteenth consecutive season in the Premier League. It ended with Chelsea earning its fourth league title by just one point. The team won 27 of its 38 games, with a total of 103 goals scored. Notable games included a 5–0 win over

SPORT SHORT
The 1930 soccer movie *The Great Game* starred several Chelsea players.

Anticipation floods the crowd just before Didier Drogba scores a goal.

Blackburn Rovers, 4–0 over Wolverhampton Wanderers, and a 7–0 win over Stoke City. Just one week after the final Premier League match of the season—an 8–0 win over Wigan Athletic—Chelsea faced Portsmouth in the FA Cup final at Wembley Stadium. The stands were filled, while millions more watched live on television. Didier Drogba scored the winning goal in the fifty-eighth minute. Team captain John Terry would later say that the pitch at Wembley had been the worst he had played on all year. Pitch quality aside, it was a proud day for Chelsea when the players lifted the cup, doubly so because of their earlier Premier League win. Many fans still consider this season one of the best since Roman Abramovich took over the team. The coach that guided the team to the double victory was Carlo Ancelotti. He was fired one year later, a reminder that a team manager's fate changes quickly.

THE CHELSEA FOUNDATION

The Chelsea Foundation was started in 2010. It organizes and participates in many charitable programs, both at home and overseas. Its main goal is to use "the power of the football to motivate, educate, and inspire." Through its programs, it talks about issues such as education, antidiscrimination, lowering crime, and employment. Every year, one Foundation participant receives the Peter Osgood Award. It is given out for good work.

Since 2015, the Foundation has joined Plan International, a global children's charity that works to provide better education and living conditions in developing countries. Together, they have created a project to help boys and girls in Colombia go to school, have clean water, and get medicine when they need it.

Meanwhile, in the United Kingdom, in addition to offering special community days and coaching events especially for women fans, one successful program has been their "Say No to Anti-Semitism" Campaign. The Foundation works with the Anne Frank Museum and other organizations to teach fans about ending discrimination and supporting Jewish communities. The team has supported special workshops about these topics at area schools. The program received the Community Project of the Year Award at the 2019 London Football Awards.

WINS AT WEMBLEY, OLD AND NEW

The 2010 FA Cup final win was Chelsea's sixth such victory. Two earlier FA Cup final wins were notable, not because they happened right after each other, but because of the stadium at which they took place. With its twin towers, London's Wembley Stadium was a much-loved national landmark. Multiple sporting events were held there, including the FA Cup final. The 2000 FA Cup final match was an emotional one for many reasons, one of the most important being that it was the last played at the stadium in its old form. Wembley closed in October 2000 and was demolished in 2002 to make way for a newer facility.

On May 20, 2000, Chelsea faced off against Aston Villa at the grounds. The first half was unremarkable

The new Wembley Stadium opened in 2007 and has room for ninety thousand soccer spectators.

for both teams, but play improved in the second half, and Roberto Di Matteo scored the only goal in the seventy-third minute.

It was only appropriate then that after winning the last FA Cup final at the old Wembley, Chelsea should win the first to be held at the new Wembley Stadium in 2007. This time, the team was paired against Manchester United. Chelsea had won the season's League Cup, while Manchester United was the Premier League Champion. The game went into extra time with Didier Drogba finally scoring in the 116th minute. The victory marked José Mourinho's first FA Cup win.

UEFA CHAMPIONS LEAGUE

Chelsea lost its first UEFA Champions League final in 2008. However, the team got a second chance in 2012. The opponent was Bayern Munich, a four-time winner of the Champions League. To make matters tougher for Chelsea, they were playing at Munich's Allianz Arena, Bayern's home stadium. For much of the match, Chelsea was the underdog. Bayern was in control. Even so, scoring came relatively late. Bayern's Thomas Muller scored in the eighty-third minute. This seemed to spur the Chelsea players into action. Five minutes later, Drogba got a goal to make the score equal. Just before the final whistle, Drogba had a free kick, but he missed the goal, so the match went into extra time. Chelsea won 4–3 on penalties, with Drogba getting the final, and winning, point. The win was Chelsea's first European cup. It was also the first time a London team had won the Champions League—both Chelsea and Arsenal having failed on previous tries.

CHELSEA FC WOMEN

A women's team, Chelsea Ladies, first formed in 1992 and became officially affiliated with the men's team in 2004. The following year, they were promoted to the Premier Division in women's soccer and quickly became one of Britain's leading teams. In 2010, a new FA Women's Super League (WSL) was announced. The Super League is made up of the eight top teams in the nation. Chelsea was one of those eight teams when the Super League launched in 2011.

In 2015, Chelsea Ladies won the FA Women's Cup for the first time. One month later, they also won their first FA WSL championship. They went on to win both titles again in the 2017–2018 season.

Chelsea Ladies changed their name in 2018. They are now known as Chelsea FC Women. Since 2017, their home ground has been at Kingsmeadow, in the southwestern suburbs of London. Erin Cuthbert and Ji So-Yun were both nominated for Women's Player of the Year at the 2019 London Football Awards.

Chelsea Ladies (now Chelsea FC Women) celebrate their 2015 FA Cup final win.

OLD AND NEW RIVALRIES

José Mourinho joined Chelsea as manager in 2004. He coached the club during some of its most successful seasons, winning an impressive collection of titles.

During his time with the club, he placed more importance on getting results than on playing with style. Mourinho had started his career as a player in his native Portugal. His career was fairly successful but not especially memorable. In 2000, he switched careers to managing. This was where he made his mark on the soccer world. His knowledge of match tactics, his ability to spot great players, and his emphasis on results quickly made him one of the sport's leaders.

Upon his arrival at Chelsea in June 2004, he told the press, "We have the top players and … we have a top manager." He brought many of his key Portuguese coaching staff with him and brought top players to the club, including several from his former team, Porto.

He managed for three seasons, leaving in 2007, only to return in 2013. After he left Stamford Bridge for the second time in December 2015, he moved to Chelsea's Premier League rivals, Manchester United. During his first season there, United won the EFL Cup, the FA Community Shield, and the Europa League. So when the two teams met for the 2018 FA Cup final, the match

José Mourinho was one of Chelsea's most successful managers—
and one of the most controversial.

was sure to be bittersweet. On the one hand, Chelsea
had fond memories of Mourinho. On the other, he was
now coaching their rivals. Furthermore, he and the
Chelsea coach, Antonio Conte, had clashed at previous
matches. Chelsea was also keen to redeem itself after
the previous year's FA Cup final loss to Arsenal.

Chelsea's Eden Hazard scored from a penalty kick
just twenty-two minutes into the match. Although
Manchester United made several attempts to score in
the second half, the club were unable to do so. Antonio
Conte got his first domestic cup win. Meanwhile,
Mourinho lost his first ever cup final with an English
team. Chelsea had demonstrated its ability to move on.
The club's success was not tied to any one coach.

Police battle to keep rival fans apart at Stamford Bridge in 1982.

CHALLENGES FACING CHELSEA

The early 2000s brought repeated success for Chelsea, with several excellent wins and championship titles. However, there were still challenges behind the scenes. Many of these problems were not new. Instead, they had been pushed to one side. In the twenty-first century, they could no longer be ignored if Chelsea was to move forward. Over the next decade, Chelsea would continue to change, and some strong personalities would make sure the team continued to grow.

SOCCER VIOLENCE

One major problem that haunted Chelsea, particularly during the 1970s and 1980s and somewhat even now, has been hooliganism. This means bad behavior by fans at matches. By the 1970s, fighting between English fans was very common. In fact, foreign soccer teams called it "the English disease."

Soccer hooligans formed organized gangs that regularly committed acts of violence against opposing fans, as well as vandalism, or destruction of property.

The violence was often worse when local clubs played each other, as there was less distance to travel. To the gangs, the actual game itself was much less important than starting fights after the game.

The Chelsea Headhunters were one of the most well-known gangs in the world of English soccer. Their reputation became so bad that, in 1985, club owner Ken Bates installed an electric fence at Stamford Bridge to prevent fans from storming the pitch. However, he was denied permission to switch it on, so eventually he removed it.

The British government also tried to solve the problem of hooliganism. For a while, fans were banned from traveling to away games, although this was difficult to enforce. The breaking point came in May 1985, when soccer violence led to a riot and caused the deaths of thirty-nine people. This time, the Chelsea Headhunters were not involved. Liverpool fans rioted before a match in Belgium, and thirty-nine Juventus fans died in the violence. As a result, English clubs were banned from competing in other European countries for five years. Other steps were also taken around this time, including the separation of team supporters within the stands, replacing all standing areas with assigned seating, and stronger match security. These, combined with the

SPORT SHORT
Chelsea's first nickname was "the Pensioners" for the nearby army veterans' hospital. Now they are "the Blues" because of their signature blue home uniforms.

extended ban, put an end to much of the violence. Soccer became a family-friendly, Saturday afternoon event once again.

That is not to say that all soccer violence has ended, however. In 2015, video footage showed a group of Chelsea fans in Paris. They pushed a Frenchman of African descent off the Metro train and kept him from boarding. As they did so, they sang racist chants. Chelsea FC made a public statement about the behavior of the supporters, calling it "abhorrent." They said that there was no place for such actions in soccer or in society. The men in the video were later identified and faced criminal charges. All were punished with fines or lengthy bans from attending any Chelsea matches. Meanwhile, the Chelsea Foundation has worked with local schools to educate and put an end to racist violence.

AN OUTDATED STADIUM

Another problem facing Chelsea involved their beloved home ground, Stamford Bridge. When Stamford Bridge was built in 1877, it was the second-largest stadium in the country. Only London's Crystal Palace could hold more people. When they were built, a lot of the space was for people to stand. Newer safety rules, however, said that it was too dangerous for so many people to be squeezed into one place. Rows of seats were installed. These were more comfortable, but they meant that fewer people could attend games. Fewer people meant less money, and times were changing. In the 1970s, the team's owners wanted to rebuild Stamford Bridge. The plan was to make it bigger and more modern. It would

GLOBAL SPONSORSHIP DEALS

In the twenty-first century, a series of sponsorship deals have helped make Chelsea into a global brand. In 2015, a five-year shirt sponsorship contract was signed between Chelsea and Japanese tire manufacturer Yokohama Rubber. The Yokohama name is printed on the front of all players' shirts. Soccer is very popular in Japan and Korea. Using a Japanese company's name as a sponsor is proof of how popular Chelsea FC is overseas.

One year later, the team announced that it was ending its partnership with sports label Adidas in favor of a new fifteen-year deal with Nike. The new deal, at more than $1 billion dollars, is worth more than double the Adidas sponsorship.

Yokohama Rubber has been a major sponsor of Chelsea since 2015.

A third major sponsorship deal was announced in 2018, when Korean carmaker Hyundai became the team's official global automotive partner. For four years, starting with the 2018–2019 season, the Hyundai logo will appear on the left sleeve of team shirts worn at home matches.

have room for more people, and even a restaurant and a hotel. These plans did not happen because they were so expensive. By the 2000s, Chelsea's debts had grown. One way to tackle debt would be to have a larger stadium that could attract more people, but to build a larger stadium, a lot of money was needed.

Although Chelsea FC wanted to build a bigger stadium at Stamford Bridge, the team did not own the ground. A group of businessmen had bought it in the 1970s so that they could remodel it. Instead, they had failed. By 1992, the company that owned Stamford Bridge owed too much money and declared bankruptcy. This meant that banks now owned the stadium. They would need to sell it to raise enough money to pay the debts. Chelsea chairman Ken Bates had another idea. He created the Chelsea Pitch Owners (CPO), a nonprofit organization that would manage Stamford Bridge. The CPO is made up of Chelsea fans. Anyone can become a member by giving some money. In 1997, the CPO bought the stadium from the bank. They also bought the naming rights to Chelsea Football Club. This made sure that the ground could never again be resold. Also, no one person can now decide what happens to the stadium. Furthermore, if the soccer club moves to a new stadium location, they cannot call themselves Chelsea Football Club without permission from the CPO. The CPO has helped to protect the stadium. It also caused some arguments with owner Roman Abramovich. In October 2011, the club wanted to buy the stadium back from the CPO. Financially, Chelsea was much more stable. It no longer had all of the debts that it used to owe. Abramovich said that there was no longer a need for separate ownership. However, 75 percent of the CPO needed to agree to any decisions before they could be made. Only 61 percent voted in favor. The following year, Chelsea FC tried to buy the abandoned ground of Battersea Power Station. They wanted to build a new stadium on the site. Again, the CPO had to approve continuing to use the Chelsea name. Plans eventually fell through.

FINANCIAL HURDLES AND A SAVIOR

The club had been having financial troubles for quite some time by the early 2000s. Chelsea had lots of legal battles and spent too much money buying top players. However, there was a significant turn of events in 2003 that would help secure Chelsea's future.

In July of that year, newspapers said a young Russian billionaire had bought Chelsea FC. Politician, investment company owner, and philanthropist Roman Abramovich was unknown to soccer fans. The announcement that he now owned the club was met with doubt. Who was he? What were his plans?

Abramovich immediately spent large amounts of money to invest in Chelsea's future. He spent more than £100 million ($133 million) on players for the new season, one of the biggest purchases in world soccer. This included talent

Roman Abramovich has owned Chelsea FC since 2003.

ARSENAL: RIVAL TEAMS, RIVAL MANAGERS

Arsenal and Chelsea share a fierce rivalry on the soccer pitch.

The existing rivalry between Chelsea and Arsenal became much more intense during José Mourinho's years as manager. This was due to the tensions between him and long-time Arsenal coach Arsène Wenger.

Although both teams have their homes in London, their rivalry intensified in the 2000s as Chelsea became more prominent and rose in the Premier League. As the teams fought for dominance, Mourinho and Wenger were both highly outspoken and often critical of each other. In October 2014, there was a physical confrontation during a match at Stamford Bridge. Wenger pushed Mourinho in the chest, and a match official had to calm things down. Since Wenger's retirement in 2018, both have admitted their respect for the other.

Although Chelsea won the teams' first meeting in 1907, Arsenal has won more of their matches against each other. With management changes, the rivalry continues, but perhaps more calmly.

from both England and overseas. He bought players from Italy and Spain and set a new record for the club when he bought Irish wing Damien Duff for £17 million ($22.5 million).

The spending spree quickly paid off. For the first time in eleven years, Chelsea scored their first Premiership game win at Liverpool's Anfield Stadium. (The team had beaten Liverpool during this time but not in an away match at Liverpool's home ground.) In November 2003, a 4–0 win over Lazio in Rome and a 1–0 win against Manchester United helped earn Chelsea a position as a leader in European soccer. The club's Champions League quarterfinal win marked their first defeat of Arsenal in seventeen games. The team was performing well. Now, the players needed to repeat these wins and to win trophies every season, not just every two or three years.

NEW SUCCESSES

Abramovich's strategy was to hire José Mourinho. Mourinho's first season in 2004–2005 was Chelsea's most successful ever to that point. After an opening day win against Manchester United, the team went on to win the League Championship against Liverpool. Chelsea's success continued through the next few years under Mourinho's guidance. The team won the FA Community Shield in 2005 and continued to set records for the number of wins in a row, least number of goals conceded in a season, and so on. They also became the first London club to win back-to-back championships since the 1930s.

Chelsea players wave during a parade in 2005 to celebrate their first league trophy in fifty years.

With Abramovich's investment in both players and management, Chelsea had become a soccer force. Behind the scenes, however, the club's debts had reached record-breaking proportions. By 2008, the club owed £736 million ($977 million). Most of the money was owed by the club to Abramovich. He had loaned millions of pounds to buy new players and to pay salaries. In 2009, Abramovich agreed to erase all of the debt that was owed to him. This move would go a long way in ensuring a stable future for Chelsea FC. It also helped to improve Chelsea's world standing. By 2011, the team was ranked the fifth most valuable club in European soccer. However, experts warned that several things were standing in its way of becoming a truly global brand. One factor was a lack of recent trophy wins. After Mourinho's departure in 2007, there had been many coaches, most staying barely one season. The team needed leadership that would stick around. Another factor was the stadium size, which was still limiting growth. The people in charge of Chelsea would not allow these challenges to hold them back. Instead, they would work even harder to grow.

The team celebrates the Capital One Cup final victory over Tottenham Hotspur in 2015.

THE CLUB'S LEGACY

For so many decades after its creation in 1905, Chelsea FC was entertaining and popular with local fans, but the team never reached the success it desired. In that respect, Chelsea is, despite its age, a relatively young team. Its success has happened largely in the last twenty years or so. Since Roman Abramovich bought the club in 2003, its rise to global celebrity status has been swift and shows few signs of slowing.

GROWING AS A GLOBAL CLUB

In 2012, the club that was once famous for its debt made a profit for the first time in years. In addition to making an overall profit of £1.4 million ($1.9 million), the club also had a record income of £255.7 million ($339 million). This made them the fifth-largest club in Europe in terms of income. The year 2012 was full of more than financial success. The team also won the UEFA Champions League and their fourth FA Cup in six years. These on-pitch victories, in turn, led to an increase of revenue.

Antonio Conte was the manager of Chelsea FC from 2016 to 2018.

Chelsea continued to build on that success the following year, joining AFC Ajax, Bayern Munich, and Juventus in becoming one of the only teams to have won all three major UEFA Cup competitions.

In terms of club value, Chelsea has remained consistent at the sixth- or seventh-place ranking when compared with other European clubs.

COACH TURNOVER

However, coach turnover, or the number of coaches leaving and joining the club, has remained a problem. José Mourinho returned for a brief period from 2013 to 2015. In 2015, he was named Premier League Manager of the Season, after Chelsea lost just three games. He was also named Portuguese Coach of the Century by the Portuguese Football Federation. Despite signing a contract to stay at Chelsea until 2019, José Mourinho announced his move to Manchester United in 2016.

Since his departure, the club has had many replacements. Antonio Conte joined in July 2016. He was the third coach in just seven months since Mourinho's departure. Within two years, his future was in doubt. Many problems had fans calling for him to be fired, including a meager two wins in a ten-match period and public arguments that led to star striker

Diego Costa leaving. To make things worse, Conte told the press that he was more interested in going home to Italy than he was in leading Chelsea to a Champions League win. His dismissal in July 2018 was not a huge surprise.

Despite the problems with management, 2018 was not a bad year for Chelsea. The team continued to be ranked the seventh strongest and most valuable brand in soccer. FA Cup final successes and strong new players added to the team's value.

REDEVELOPMENT?

One problem continued: stadium size at Stamford Bridge. It had been a long-standing barrier to the club's growth. By January 2017, Chelsea was ready to build a new stadium at Stamford Bridge. Permission was needed from the mayor of London and from the

Stamford Bridge has been Chelsea FC's home since the club's founding in 1905.

transport networks, but once that was given, plans for a new sixty-thousand-seat stadium were finally underway. After years of negotiating, the Chelsea Pitch Owners and Abramovich reached an agreement at their meeting in January 2017.

Everyone knew that Chelsea's long-term success depended on being able to have more fans attend games. Increasing the number of seats in the stadium would bring more people in and raise more money. Figures showed that a new stadium, in fact, would double income over a ten-year period, further securing the financial future of the team. Renovating seemed like the best path to take.

To still be able to practice and play home games, the team would need a temporary stadium for three to four years while construction happened. Wembley seemed like an option, and Chelsea would possibly share it for a while with Tottenham, whose ground was also undergoing renovation.

At first, it was thought Chelsea would be back in their new stadium by the 2021–2022 season. However, this was later pushed back to 2023 to allow for additional changes to nearby underground railway stations.

Fans were both surprised and disappointed when an unexpected announcement came in May 2018. The redevelopment plans had been put on hold due to the "current unfavorable investment climate." Chelsea was still playing at Stamford Bridge in 2019, and all construction plans had stopped. It is unknown if or when redevelopment will continue.

NEW COACH, NEW ERA

Maurizio Sarri took over managing Chelsea on July 14, 2018, one day after Antonio Conte was fired. He was a former banker and amateur player until 1999 when he began pursuing a full-time career as coach. His start with Chelsea was perhaps not the best; the team lost its Community Shield match to Manchester City. However, he then went on to see twelve successive league wins.

Manager Maurizio Sarri calls out to players during a match in 2019.

Even so, soccer is a sport that changes a lot. Fans and owners are happy as long as the team keeps winning. One loss is often not much of a problem. More than that, though, and a coach's future with the team becomes unclear. Rumors began about Sarri's future in spring 2019. Chelsea faced three Premier League losses against Arsenal (2–0), Bournemouth (4–0), and Manchester City (6–0). Premier League wins against Huddersfield, Spurs, and Fulham helped, but not by much.

The Fulham match was of particular interest since it was goalkeeper Kepa Arrizabalaga's first game since the February 2019 Carabao Cup (League Cup) match against Manchester City. In the Carabao Cup match, Sarri had attempted to substitute Kepa, as he is known, before a penalty shootout to decide the fate of the match. The goalkeeper refused to leave the pitch. He later apologized, and Sarri claimed the whole event had been a misunderstanding. Still, the player was fined a week's wages and was left out of Chelsea's next match. Kepa is the world's most expensive goalkeeper, but his bad temper has some fans thinking he shouldn't be on the team.

Such ups and downs are part of the world of soccer. Maurizio Sarri has said he intends to lead Chelsea back to the top of the Champions League.

PLAYERS IN PROGRESS

In terms of players, the future looks bright for Chelsea. The youth teams that Ted Drake created in the 1950s continue to develop young talent and are considered the best in the country. Current Chelsea stars Ruben

Are these tomorrow's soccer stars? Members of the Chelsea FC Under-19 youth team pose for the camera in 2019.

Loftus-Cheek, Ethan Ampadu, and Andreas Christensen all moved up from the youth team. Many others are expected to play for Chelsea in the coming seasons. The club also brings in players from other English and European teams, always trying to build a better and stronger force.

With a roster of world-class players and the financial support of owner Abramovich, it looks as though the future of Chelsea will continue to be filled with trophies, victory, and excitement for the club's loyal fans.

1905   Chelsea Football Club is founded and is elected to Division Two of the English Football League. Its first competitive match is played.

1915   Chelsea reaches its first FA Cup final.

1955   Chelsea wins its first Division Championship and FA Charity Shield.

1965   Chelsea has its first League Cup win.

1970   Chelsea wins the FA Cup and UEFA Cup Winners' Cup.

1997   Chelsea wins the FA Cup.

1998   Chelsea wins the League Cup and UEFA Cup Winners' Cup. The team becomes UEFA Super Cup Champions.

2000   Chelsea wins the FA Cup and FA Charity Shield.

2003   Russian billionaire Roman Abramovich makes a surprise purchase of Chelsea FC.

2004   José Mourinho takes over as team manager.

2005   Chelsea wins the League Cup and Community Shield. The team also becomes the Premier League Champion.

2006   Chelsea becomes the Premier League Champion again.

2007   Chelsea wins the League Cup and FA Cup. José Mourinho departs.

2009   Chelsea wins the FA Cup and FA
       Community Shield.

2010   Chelsea wins the the FA Cup and
       becomes Premier League Champion.

2012   Chelsea wins the FA Cup and becomes
       UEFA Champions League Champion.

2013   Chelsea wins the UEFA Europe League
       Championship. José Mourinho returns as
       team manager.

2015   Chelsea wins the League Cup and
       becomes the Premier League Champion.
       José Mourinho leaves again.

2017   Chelsea becomes the Premier
       League Champion.

2018   Maurizio Sarri replaces Antonio Conte as
       manager. Chelsea wins the FA Cup.

anti-Semitism A set of racist beliefs and prejudice against Jewish people.

charitable Helping someone in need.

concede To give up. In the case of soccer, to allow your opponent to score a goal.

CPO Chelsea Pitch Owners; a group of Chelsea fans and supporters who invested in ownership of Stamford Bridge to protect it from future sale or unapproved redevelopment.

extra time An extra thirty minutes of play, often used in championship games or competition stages when the match has resulted in a tie.

FA Cup The Football Association Challenge Cup; a knockout tournament in English soccer.

goodwill tour A visit to many countries that is intended to improve friendliness between people or countries.

hooliganism Disruptive and violent behavior, usually carried out by organized gangs at sporting events.

league A group of sports teams that play regular competitive matches against each other.

nouveau riche From the French, meaning "new rich," it is often used to describe someone who has recently become wealthy and is used in a slightly insulting way to suggest that the person has money but no taste.

penalty kick A free kick awarded when a foul by the defending team occurs inside the penalty box. The ball is placed twelve yards from goal with only the opposing team's goalie to defend it.

penalty shootout A way of deciding the winner of a championship match if the result is still a tie after extra time has been played. Players on each team take turns shooting at the goal, with the team with the most goals out of five attempts winning, unless it's a tie, in which case it goes to additional rounds until there is a winner.

Premier League The top level of English football, consisting of twenty teams that can be promoted or relegated based upon performance.

refurbishment The redecorating and sometimes rebuilding of something to make more modern.

relegation The process of being sent to a lower league due to bad results in a soccer season.

season The months of the year when soccer is played. The Premier League usually begins in mid-August and continues until mid-May.

sponsorship Financial support from a company, often with an expectation in return. For example, Yokohama Tires pays a large amount of money to Chelsea, and in return, their logo is displayed on all team shirts.

Stamford Bridge The home ground of Chelsea Football Club, located in the Hammersmith and Fulham neighborhood of London.

stands Tiered rows for spectators at a sporting arena.

striker A forward player who is often most responsible for scoring goals.

UEFA The Union of European Football Associations; an administrative organization representing soccer in Europe.

BOOKS

Antill, David, Josh James, and Match! Magazine. *The Official Chelsea FC Annual 2019*. London, UK: Aspen Books, 2019.

Chelsea FC. *Chelsea FC: Premier League Champions 2017*. London, UK: Trinity Mirror Sport Media, 2017.

Glanvill, Rick, and Paul Dutton. *Chelsea: The Complete Record*. London, UK: DeCoubertin Books, 2015.

O'Neill, Michael. *Chelsea: A Backpass Through History*. Solihull, UK: Danann Publishing, 2017.

WEBSITES

Official Chelsea Website

http://www.chelseafc.com

This is the official Chelsea soccer club website, featuring team information, stats, history, and more.

Premier League Chelsea

https://www.premierleague.com/clubs/4/Chelsea/overview

Here you can find club information and Chelsea's current standings within the Premier League.

UEFA Chelsea

https://www.uefa.com/teamsandplayers/teams/club=52914/profile/index.html

This site includes team statistics and championship records, as well as other information about the Union of European Football Associations (UEFA).

World Football

https://www.worldfootball.net

Find up-to-date news about matches and transfers in the international soccer world at this website.

VIDEOS

Chelsea FC Video Collection

https://www.chelseafc.com/en/videos

Match highlights, club news, and exclusive interviews with players and managers are found here.

Chelsea FC YouTube Channel

https://www.youtube.com/user/chelseafc/videos?flow=grid&sort=dd&view=0

Chelsea's YouTube channel is regularly updated with video interviews and match clips.

SELECTED BIBLIOGRAPHY

Beasley, Robert. *José Mourinho: Up Close and Personal.* London, UK: Michael O'Mara, 2017.

Chelsea FC. *Chelsea Uncut: Inside the Bridge.* London, UK: Trinity Mirror Sport Media, 2019.

Donovan, Mike. *Chelsea On This Day: History, Facts, & Figures From Every Day of the Year.* Worthing, UK: Pitch Publishing, 2013.

Folgar, Carlos, and Deborah W. Crisfield. *The Everything Kids' Soccer Book: Rules, Techniques, and More About Your Favorite Sport!* New York, NY: Everything Books, 2018.

Gifford, Clive. *The Kingfisher Soccer Encyclopedia.* New York, NY: Kingfisher, 2018.

Glanvill, Rick. *Chelsea FC: The Official Biography – The Definitive Story of the First 100 Years.* London, UK: Headline Press, 2006.

Hamilton, Duncan. *Going to the Match.* London, UK: Hodder & Stoughton, 2018.

Harris, Harry. *Ruud Gullit: The Chelsea Diary.* London, UK: Orion, 1997.

Hopcraft, Arthur. *The Football Man: People & Passions in Soccer.* London, UK: Aurum Press, 2013.

Mantz, Gabriel. *Yearbook of European Football 2018–2019.* Cleethorpes, UK: Soccer Books Ltd., 2018.

Midgley, Dominic, and Chris Hutchins. *Abramovich: The Billionaire From Nowhere.* London, UK: James Leasor Publishing, 2015.

Mourinho, José. *Mourinho.* London, UK: Headline, 2015.

Murray, Scott. *The Title: The Story of the First Division.* London, UK: Bloomsbury Sport, 2017.

Tesser, Greg. *Chelsea FC in the Swinging '60s: Football's First Rock'n'Roll Club*. Stroud, UK: The History Press, 2013.

Williams, Heather. *Chelsea FC: Inside Professional Soccer*. New York, NY: Av2, 2019.

Woolnough, Brian. *Glenn Hoddle: The Man and the Manager*. London, UK: Virgin Books, 1997.

INDEX

Page numbers in **boldface** are images.

ABOUT THE AUTHOR

Fiona Young-Brown is the author of more than a dozen books, including *Dilemmas in Democracy: Fake News and Propaganda* and *Great Discoveries in Science: Plate Tectonics.* Other topics she enjoys writing about include the history of Kentucky, food, travel, and great apes. Originally from England and a family of Arsenal supporters, Young-Brown now lives in Lexington, Kentucky, with her husband and dog.